SPEED

READING

The Ultimate Guide to Mastering Reading with Speed That Will Boost Your Productivity and Make You Successful

Author: John Slavio

TABLE OF CONTENTS

DISCLAIMER

ABOUT THE AUTHOR

John Slavio is a programmer who is passionate about the reach of the internet and the interaction of the internet with daily devices. He has automated several home devices to make them 'smart' and connect them to high speed internet. His passions involve computer security, iOT, hardware programming and blogging. Below is a list of his books:

John Slavio Special

INTRODUCTION

Imagine if you had a few extra hours every week. How would you use them? Would you finally do all the things that get endlessly postponed? If you want a workday's worth of extra time on a weekly basis, then you have definitely landed at the right place.

This is a book that will not only save you a lot of time, but it will also make you function more efficiently. It will boost your productivity and put you in the lane to success. No, I am not selling some magical product. I am merely teaching what most successful people already know.

Most of the successful people don't just read, they soak information like sponges. Their eyes and brain are trained to run smoothly as a unit that results in enhanced focus and increased comprehension. Say goodbye to wasting your time reading meaningless emails and documents, because this book will turn you into a 'sponge'.

From how you can benefit from speed reading to teaching you the most successful techniques that will help you master this skill-of-the-successful in no time, this book will drag much more values than extra time into your world.

Are you ready for the change?

What Kind of a Reader Are You?

Before I delve deeply into revealing to you the ultimate tricks and tips of speed reading, you must first determine exactly where you stand as a speed reader. No, I will not ask you to read "War and Peace". This next exercise will only take a minute of your time. It takes only a minute for you to see how badly you need to read this book. Thanks to this next one-minute exercise you might boost your productivity permanently.

In this exercise, we will see exactly how fast of a reader you are by determining the average number of words you read per minute.

1. Choose any article to read for this exercise.
2. Have a timing device nearby.
3. Set the timer to go off after one minute passes.
4. Press 'start' and begin reading.
5. Stop reading exactly after one minute.
6. Mark the line you are on.
7. Count the number of words from the first five rows and divide that number by 5. That is the average number of words per line.
8. Now, count the number of lines you have read.

Your reading WPM (words per minute) rate can be determined by simply multiplying the number of lines read by the average number of words per line:

<u>Number of lines x Words per line = WPM</u>

Now that you know your reading WPM, let's check out the results and see how fast of a reader you are:

< 200 WPM. If you have managed to read less than 200 words per minute, then you are what they call *talkers*. You read a sentence with the same speed it takes you to say the words out loud. You read only one word at a time, and when reading fast (and comprehending!) you may hit 240 WPM. There are very few of the *talkers* who can actually hit a 400 WPM.

You are a talker because you can actually hear yourself read. You engage in the *vocalization* as you read, and that is a habit that slows you down extremely.

200-300 WPM. If you have read somewhere between 200 and 300 words per minute, then you are an average reader. The average readers do not enjoy reading particularly, and reading books is not their hobby. Unfortunately, most people fall under this category. These are the people that haven't had reading trainings since they were in elementary school.

However, belonging in this category is nothing to be ashamed off. Being an average reader does not mean that you do not read at all. Most lawyers and doctors are average readers and they read all the time.

The average readers also engage in vocalization, but they are also capable of reading a couple of different words at once.

300 to 700 WPM. People who read from 300 to 700 words are considered to be *above-average readers*. They can easily read groups of words at once, as well as recognize phrases in sentences at a single glance. The above-average readers engage very little in vocalization, are well-educated and most likely have a pretty large vocabulary.

>700 WPM. If you have read more than 700 words in one minute, then you already are a speed reader. You do not vocalize, and can easily read up to 15 words at one glance.

Although speed readers do not really need to read speed-reading books, don't throw this book on your read-for-later-book pile. Who knows, maybe you will learn a new technique that you are unfamiliar with and increase your agility even more. Besides, it will take less than 13 minutes of your time to get to the final page.

Another way for you to test your speed reading rate is to simply measure yourself reading 700 words. After you are done, simply divide 700 by the time that it took you to read them and you will get your WPM. For example, if you read 700 words in 2.75 minutes, your speed reading WPM is 700/2.75 = 254.5

Understanding Speed Reading

You read a book. By the time you get to the middle of the page you 'wake up' just to realize that you haven't been paying any attention. Sound familiar? That is what happens with 'regular reading'; the mind wanders. And while not paying attention to how Khaleesi ended up riding the dragon while reading the new 'Game of Thrones' book may not have a significant impact on your life, to have your mind wandered while reading an important document at work might actually hurt your work position. So why not try a new, much more efficient method of reading?

Contrary to the popular belief that speed reading is a whole different reading technique, it actually isn't. You cannot change reading. You see the words, you inhale the information. However, you can change the attention you pay while reading, and that is what speed reading is all about really. Unlike 'regular reading', speed reading is a much more focused way of reading.

Speed Reading Equals Seeing

People in the past believed that reading was moving the eyes from left to right, seeing one word at a time. But no one (except for those who are just learning how to read) can see only one word at a time. You can check your eye fixations by simply focusing on a single word, As you can see, you don't see only one word. You also see those surrounding that word. As you move your eyes across the lines, they move into starts and fits and can easily soak up to five words.

Speed reading can help you increase this ability by:

- Helping you read a couple of words at once. Unless you bump into an unfamiliar word, your eyes will jump that way that they will absorb multiple words at a single glance.
- Expanding your vision. Not only does speed reading let you see multiple words as one, but it also trains you to process and understand them at the same time.
- Expanding your vision to see not only horizontally, but vertically too. Do you know that speed readers read and understand words from 2 or 3 lines all at once?

Speed Reading Equals Silent Reading

Can you hear yourself talk while you read? Is there a voice coming from the page? Don't worry, most people hear a whispering when they read. But why is that? People can actually 'hear' the read words because they were trained to read that way. Remember how your teachers in school used to teach you that letters could make sounds and by combining those 'sounds' you could actually pronounce real words? And while this may be a great technique that allows kids to learn how to read, it is also what will slow down their reading later on in life. You may not be opening your mouth or saying the words out load, but whispering them in your head takes the exact same time.

Speed reading will train you how to read faster by not sounding the words out. Why Speed Reading? It may seem impossible now, but this book will definitely help you master that technique.

Speed Reading Equals Comprehension

What would you enjoy more, to watch a movie from the beginning to the end in one day, or to watch it in 15-minute segments all week? After watching the movie for 7 days would you still be able to grasp the whole context and meaning of the story? Not very likely. The same goes with reading. How many times has it happened to you to find yourself confused by a book's plot? When reading impartially, in segments, the meaning of the content fades away. But why do we read partially? Mainly because we don't have the time. Speed reading will not only give you the time to fully enjoy and understand a book, but it will also increase your ability to comprehend.

- By reading multiple words at once, you basically pick up the meaning of their context. Doing so will improve your comprehension because the words you read will give meaning to the ones that follow.
- Reading faster means reading more, and reading more leads to a larger vocabulary. The larger your vocabulary is, the more able to comprehend the context you are.

Speed Reading Equals Concentration

Sure, all reading requires concentration. Even when you read a sappy romantic short read during your holiday break, you need to have a certain level of concentration. However, speed reading requires more than simply paying attention to what you read. Speed reading requires forceful concentration of the words you read, while staying attentive of the context that the author wants to be present in the book. Speed reading is paying attention to pin down the ideas in order to be able to detach the details from the heavier stuff you read.

Speed reading means being hungry for reading and doing it aggressively.

Disproving the Common Myths

There are many myths that are associated with speed reading. From "haste makes waste" to "it is impossible to read that fast", people tend to slander this technique and maybe discourage others from taking a shot at enhancing their productivity.

Here are the most common misbeliefs about speed reading and why they are nothing more but myths:

People Cannot Enjoy Speed Reading

On the contrary, people are actually better readers when they use this technique. They fully comprehend and get the meaning of the context and can therefore enjoy the reading much more than those who read the regular way.

People Skip Words When Speed Reading

First of all, skipping words is not reading. It is omitting. And to debunk this myth, no, speed reading is not skipping words. Just because the speed reader does not focus the eyes on each word separately, doesn't mean that he skips words. His brain is just trained to pick up the context 'on the go' in order for him to be much more efficient.

People Must Use Their Fingers to Speed Read

Sure, people can use their fingers in the early stages of speed reading to jumpstart this technique, as I will talk about later on. However, that does not mean that all speed readers read that way. Some people skip the whole – finger-down-the-page method all together. So, here is yet another myth.

Why Speed Reading?

No matter what we do for a living or how well educated or financially stable we are, we all have only 24 hours each day. Some do less, some more, but the point is that each and every one of us has some obligations. Unfortunately, the modern world we live in just keeps adding to our pile of daily schedules, and most of the time, we are not only busy but overloaded with things to get done.

You must be thinking, "Okay, but how can speed reading help me with my busy daily schedules". The truth is, speed reading can do so much more for you than simply reading your email in a jiffy.

Have you ever given the reading process a thought? When we read, we engage not only our eyes, but also our ears, mouth, and most importantly, our brain. Now, imagine if you could find a way to engage these senses of yours even more? You would be much more efficient. And if that isn't a strong enough argument that will convince you to jump on the speed-reading train, then perhaps this next list of benefits will make you consider giving speed reading a fair shot:

Speed Reading Increases Confidence

The fear of being judged often sets us back. The worry of not getting the facts right often prevents us from speaking our minds. Learning how to speed read means getting more reading done. It means reading every story from your newspaper on your way to work. It means being updated and knowledgeable - skills that will make you a lot more confident. Imagine all of the topics that you will be able to discuss when meeting new people. Imagine being confident to handle your boss' questions. Imagine sharing your opinions freely on business meetings.

Speed Reading Enhances the Memory

Speed reading will not only help you read books and documents faster; it will also increase your ability to remember things. It will improve your memory not only to recognize phrases while reading, but to that extetd that you can actually use this enhanced ability in other areas in your life, as well.

Speed Reading Increases Your Focus

If you have trouble keeping yourself focused on tasks, then learning to speed read will definitely make you more efficient, even if you are performing more than a single task at once. Like we said, speed reading increases your concentration, and after a while, paying focused attention will come almost automatically to you. By speed reading you will train your brain to be more focused, which will also help you reduce the stress levels significantly.

Speed Reading Boosts Ambition

With increased focus, enhanced ability to memorize things and high confidence, you will no longer be afraid of challenging tasks. Quite the opposite, you will be much more inspired to climb higher and achieve more. With every benefit that speed reading will provide you with you will have improved ambition to set higher goals for yourself.

Now that you know what benefits speed reading can bring to your life and (hopefully!) have become even more motivated to master this skill, then it is time for us to get started learning this amazing technique.

Getting Started

Like I said, speed reading is a skill that allows you to read while paying more attention, not a whole new way of reading. To speed read, you don't need to gear yourself up with special equipment. The only things that you have to have with you are your reading material (book, computer, magazine) and your focus. Okay, and maybe a pacer (which we will talk about later on).

Here is how you can prepare yourself to learn this technique:

No Distractions. Imagine you have to study for a really important exam. Would you do it in a crowded, noisy place? I highly doubt that. Most people need a quiet, properly-lit place to be able to concentrate on the material. Speed reading, just like studying for an exam requires a place where you will be free of distractions and able to fully focus.

Turn off the TV, your phone, and tell people around you not to disturb you. You will most likely call it a day if you are distracted more than once. Avoid distractions and keep your focus sharp.

Know Your Goal. No matter what you are about to start in your life, having a goal in mind to keep you motivated is the key to success. The same goes with speed reading. It will be much easier for you to master the skill if you know why you are trying to learn it in the first place. Without that, speed reading will be one of the many pointless endeavors that people start for no particular reason.

When you try to boost your running condition, you set your goal higher each day. Today, I will run a mile. Tomorrow 1.2 miles. Then a mile and a half, then maybe two, and so on until I become able to run for 5 miles without stopping. When speed reading, you must also strive to enhance your ability until you reach your goal. So if your goal is to learn how to read 750 words per minute, I highly recommend you to remind yourself of that number so you don't fall off the track.

Visualize. Many successful people have said that the key to their achievement is their ability to visualize success before even accomplishing it. So, before you start reading, imagine yourself doing it. Imagine yourself going through the pile of documents on your desk three times faster. Imagine yourself getting more work done in the same time. Wouldn't that be something?

Breaking the Poor-Reading-Habits Cycle

We said that speed reading is an ability to pay more attention to the reading material which will result in faster, more comprehensive reading. But that is only half of what speed reading is. If learning and implementing the new method make one side of the speed reading coin, then getting rid of your old reading habits is the other. Only when you break the habits that prevent you from reading faster can you really learn how to do it.

Vocalization

Vocalization is listening to yourself talk while you read. It means hearing the words written on the page. And since we said how hearing the words is a habit that only slows down your reading, it is time to learn how to break it so we can move forward with this technique.

Let us first do a small exercise. Choose a small paragraph to read. As you read, listen closely. See if there is any movement of your tongue and lips. Can you hear the words? Based on whether they vocalize or not, there are three types of readers:

- Motor readers – they move their lips as they read. They are slow readers, read word-by-word and their average rate is 150-200 WPM.
- Auditory readers – they can still hear themselves read, but they do not engage their lips and tongues. They are skillful readers and read about 200-400 WPM.

- Visual readers – they do not vocalize or do it very minimally. Their reading rate is over 400 WPM.

Do you vocalize? If so, read on to get rid of that destructive habit.

Read for Meaning, not Sound. It may sound confusing, but to read for meaning is almost the same as to listen to someone speak. Let's imagine that you are listening to your colleague talking about his ideas for the new project. Can you hear the words? Or can you hear his description and ideas for the project?

When you listen to someone speaking, yes, you can hear the words but only in connection with the speaker's thoughts. That is what reading without hearing the words is. You can see the words but you don't need to whisper them in your head. Instead, you instantly respond to their meaning.

Think of it this way, when you were a kid, how did you learn to read? Syllable by syllable. But you don't do it now. Why? Because now you are able to recognize the words at single glance. The same way, reading without vocalizing is the ability to pick up the meaning, not the sound of the words.

Stop the Motor. If you are a motor reader, you will indeed have much more work to do than auditory readings, simply because, you will first need to learn how to stop your lips from moving before all else. However challenging that seems, with the right training, you can jump to the second category of readers in no time.

The best approach is quite simple (and delicious!) – chewing a gum. Many people have found chewing gum while reading to be a very effective way of learning how not to move the lips. However, if that cannot stop your lips from making movements, you might want to place a pen between them as you read. This will keep them from moving.

Hush Your Inner Voice. Although to stop hearing yourself read may seem like an impossible thing to do, these next techniques can indeed help you quiet your voice from within:

- See the words as symbols. Try to imagine that every word you see is a symbol. A combination of a couple of letters that have a meaning. Try to pick up the meaning by seeing that 'symbol' not hearing the word.
- Try to see more words in a line. By expanding the vision you can instantly pick up the context and not have that much time for vocalization.
- Count from one to ten repeatedly. By counting silently you will occupy your motor-vocal system and your mind will not be able to vocalize. Now, in the beginning you will most likely hear both words and numbers, but do not give up. This is by far the best approach to force yourself to stop vocalizing.

Regression

Regression is re-reading. It is going backwards and reading the words you have already read for the second time. Sometimes, regression is necessary, like reading a hard-to-decipher technical paper. Sometimes it is the author's fault. However, most of the time regression happens as a habit people use to assure that they read the words right. Obviously rereading not slows down your reading rate by half, but it also interrupts your reading flow and makes you lose your focus.

The best way to stop skipping back to words, is to simply cover them. If regression is a habit of yours, then I highly suggest you take an index card or something else that is long enough to cover the lines of your text. After you finish reading the line, cover it with the card. That way you will not be able to regress, unless you absolutely have to.

It goes without saying that concentration also pays a huge part in this. If you are not focused enough you will need to go back and reread because you are not paying enough attention to get the meaning of the text. Increasing the concentration and getting rid of distraction is another way of prevention regression from happening.

The Pacer

The pacer is a visual guide. It can be a blank card or it can be your finger. Whatever object you choose to be your 'pointer', that is your pacer. That is not an unfamiliar method. After all, most of us learned how to read with the help of our fingers. Just because of that, many people believe that the pacer is an ineffective method since it supports slow recognition of the words, not speed reading. However, that is not true at all. Using a pacer can be quite beneficial actually:

- The pacer helps your eyes focus on a particular line or group of words.
- It improves the concentration
- It directs the pathway in which your eyes move
- The pacer guides your eyes to find the next group of words accurately.
- It keeps you alert
- All in all, the pacer allows you to speed read

But just because the pacer can help you become skilled at this technique does not mean that you would be totally dependent on it. You don't have to use your pacer all the time and with every material you read. There is no trick here really. Once you learn how to speed read with the pacer, your brain and eyes will automatically read quickly and you will no longer need it. Think of the pacer as the training wheels on your first bike. They had helped you learn how to ride it, but after that, you didn't need them anymore.

Whether a card or a finger, the pacer can be used in many different techniques that will help you grasp the speed learning successfully. To help you accomplish that, I have divided reading with pacer into four groups: single-finger techniques, multiple-finger techniques, card techniques and ruler pacing.

Single-Finger Techniques

There is more than one way that you can use your finger as a pacer that will help you speed read. Here are five different techniques:

The Left Pointer Pull

The left pointer pull is reading while your eyes are accompanied by your index finger. It is called left pointer pull not because you will have to use your left index finger, but because you will have to pull your finger from the left side:

1. You can use either left or right hand for this method. Start by curling all your fingers except the index.
2. Place the index pointer on the left margin, underneath the first line of the text you plan on reading.
3. Start reading. When you approach the end of the line, move your finger down the left margin to the next line.

The Right Pointer Pull

The right pointer pull is basically the same method as the left pointer pull, except here, instead of pacing your finger underneath the first line on the left margin, you place it on the right. When your eyes come close to your finger, move it down the next line.

Both the left and the right pull are perfect for encouraging your eyes to move much faster.

Center Pointer Pull

If you are planning on reading a narrow newspaper or maybe a magazine, then this is probably the best technique that you can choose to learn speed reading with. It will help you keep your eyes focused on the text and it will support them to move faster.

1. Point your index finger on either hand.
2. Place the finger in the center, just under the line you plan on reading. You can also place it a few lines below so you can better expand your peripheral vision.
3. As you read and move your eyes to the left, move your finger down.
4. Make sure that your finger stays in the center.

The Z Pattern

The Z pattern is also excellent for reading newspapers and magazines.

1. Point your index finger of one of your hands.

2. Place it in the beginning of the line you plan on reading, on the left margin.

3. As you read and move your eyes to the right, drag your finger to the right at the same time.

4. When you reach the end of the line, drag your pacer diagonally down a couple of lines and place it in the beginning of a line, on the left.

5. Keeping your finger there, try to read as fast as you can to get to your finger quickly.

6. Once you get to the line where your finger is, continue reading while dragging your finger to the right as well.

7. Repeat the same.

As you can see, here, the finger moves in a way that forms a Z pattern.

The S Pattern

Although it is like the Z pattern, this technique uses rounded curves.

1. Point your index finger of one of your hands.

2. Place it underneath of the line that you want to read, in the middle.

3. As you read, move your finger across the line. Then, move it down making a curve shape ending underneath the beginning of a new line.

4. Continue moving your pacer in an S pattern.

The S pattern should underline everything you read but simply encourage your eyes to move faster.

Multiple-Finger Techniques

Unlike the single finger methods, here you use multiple fingers to learn how to speed read. The next few techniques will give you much more control over your reading.

Long Underline

This method is best for reading wide columns. In these methods, your fingers would be 'pulling' your eyes in the right direction.

1. Point your index, middle and ring finger together. Make sure to pull back your middle finger slightly so your fingers are the same length.
2. Place the fingers underneath the beginning of the line you plan on reading.
3. As you read, move your fingers really quickly towards the end of the line and then let them 'jump' underneath the next line immediately.

Your fingers must move extremely quickly so you can practice speed reading. To do so, consider letting your forearm to move your hand. Otherwise your hand might get tired pretty soon.

Short Underline

Just like the previous technique, the short underline is a method where you also must move your fingers quickly. The difference is that the short underline doesn't go all the way.

1. Again, point your index, middle and ring finger together.

2. Place them a quarter of a line away from the beginning, underneath the line you plan on reading.

3. As you read, move your fingers across the line and stop a quarter of a line from the end. So, basically, your fingers will only move across half a line – the middle.

4. Once your eyes meet your fingers, move your hand immediately underneath the next line, again, a quarter of a line from the beginning.

5. Continue moving your eyes and fingers as fast as you can.

Double-Pointer Pull

For this method, you will need both your hands:

1. Point the index fingers out of both hands.

2. Place the left pointer underneath the beginning of the line you plan on reading, and the right index underneath the end of that same line.

3. Start reading and move your eyes quickly from one fingertip to the other.

4. When you reach the right fingertip, slowly lower the pointers down the same line.

5. Keep lowering your pointers as you read.

The double-pointer pull will encourage you to move your eyes in a much faster left-to-right way. This technique is excellent for wide columns.

The Vulcan

The name Vulcan comes from Star Trek, because for this method, you have to position your hand the way Vulcans did on Star Trek. Although it is basically the same method as the double-pointer, I have decided to mention this technique as well, mainly because many people find this method to be more effective, since you use only one hand. However, I will let you be the judge of that.

Use this method for narrow columns only.

1. Close your left hand, making a fist. Then, point only the index and the pinky finger.
2. Place your pinky finger underneath the beginning of the line you plan on reading. Your index finger should be placed underneath the end of the same line.
3. As you read, move your eyes from one fingertip to the other.
4. When you reach the end of the line, quickly lower your fingers down, making sure they are positioned the same way.

Short Vulcan

The short Vulcan is the same method, except here, the pinky finger needs to be placed a third of a line from the beginning of the line you plan on reading, and your index finger should be placed a third of a line before the end of the same line. That makes this method more of a 'centered' Vulcan, as your fingers are placed underneath the middle 1/3 of the line.

Just like before, you'll have to move your fingers down as you finish reading the lines.

Open Hand Wiggle

Although it can be good for both wide and narrow columns, I believe this method is especially great for wide columns where there is a lot to read.

1. Open one of your hands and lay it over the text, with your middle finger positioned in the center of the column.
2. Start reading and wiggle your hand back and forth, making an S-like pattern.
3. Your hand should be resting comfortably.

Card Techniques

In addition to using your hands and fingers, you can also use a card to be your pacer. It is best to use a blank card since the writing on the card may distract your reading. There are two very successful speed reading methods that use blank card as a pacer:

The Regular Card Method

Many people prefer this one over the finger methods, simply because they find it a lot easier to follow a straight edge of a card, than to move their fingers across the lines.

1. Place your blank card on top of the line you plan on reading, covering the previous text. This is really important. Remember regression? Do

not place your card underneath the lines because that way you might be tempted to go back and reread the same words. Make sure that the card is wide enough to cover the whole line.

2. Start reading. Once you finish reading the line, immediately drag the card down to cover that line.

3. Keep dragging the card down to cover all the lines you read.

The Card Cutout Method

If you find yourself distracted by the text underneath and you think that it is getting in the way of you learning how to speed read, than maybe the regular card method isn't the right fit for you. If you cannot focus on moving your eyes quickly in the previous technique, I've got the perfect solution for you:

1. You can use a regular white paper for this method. Fold the paper in half and lay it over the material you plan on reading. With a pencil, mark the beginning and the end of the lines on the paper. Also, mark the height of the line.

2. Cut the paper from mark to the other about the height of the line.

3. Place your cutout paper or card over the text. Now there are only 2 lines exposed.

4. Start reading as quickly as you can and drag the card down as you finish reading to expose new lines.

The Ruler Pacing

The ruler pacing is a speed reading technique that uses a transparent ruler to help you really expand your peripheral vision and make you literally think 'outside the box'. It is a method that fixates only the words written in the middle. By reading the text partially you are forced to think beyond the meaning of the words you read and are encouraged to put together context and ideas.

You can use a two-inch transparent ruler for this exercise:

1. Place the ruler in the middle of the text you plan on reading.
2. Use a pacer that will help you move your eyes down. It can be your index finger, a card, or even a pencil. Place it underneath the beginning of the first line that is underneath the ruler.
3. When you reach the end of the text, write down the words and word groups you remember.
4. Repeat.

By making frequent stops to summarize what you have read and remembered, you will train your brain to be more organized and will improve your concentration.

Skimming and Scanning

Contrary to what most people think, skimming and scanning are not meant to be used all the time. You are not supposed to skip words while reading books, but when you are time limited and are looking through a pile of document to find some information, it would be a total waste of time to read each document word-by-word. But skimming and scanning are not only meant to be the shortcut you will take to get to information. They are also a very important step in your speed learning journey because they will also train your eyes to move in a much quicker way. Skimming and scanning require a great deal of concentration, so it is safe to say that these techniques will definitely enhance your focus and transform speed reading into a much easier task.

Skimming

Skimming is a speed reading technique that involves a really rapid movement of the eyes in order to pull out the main context of the text. When to skim?

- If you are reading some material that do not require you to pay that much attention to details, then skimming is the best way to read it, without wasting your time.
- Skimming is great for pre-reading; it is much more helpful than simple previewing because it allows you to make a more detailed picture.

- If you want to review a material that you have already read, what other method to use but to quickly skim through it?

Many people believe that skimming is a technique that does not require special training. What is there to learn about skimming, right? Well, wrong. The point of skimming is not to go through 1000 words in one minute and not get the idea. That is easy. But skimming to truly understand the context, now that is somewhat more challenging.

Like I said, skimming is a great pushing force while learning to speed read, and this is how you can master it. Let's say that you have to get the general overview of an article, but don't have the time to read the whole thing. Here is how you do it:

1. Reading the title is a must. Most authors use many important keywords in it, so make sure not to skip that part.
2. Read the first paragraph completely, but fast.
3. Read the first sentence of each paragraph.
4. Read the subheadings and try to connect the dots by creating the relation between the in your head.
5. Dip into the whole text and look for important words that may answer what, when, who, where, how, why.
6. Check the enumerations and qualifying adjectives (such as best, worst, most, least...)
7. Look for text that is underlined; Look for italics and bolds as well.
8. Read the last paragraph.

Scanning

To put it simply, a scan is a pattern of search. It is much more detailed search than skimming because while scanning you are not only looking for the main idea, but you are trying to find a specific piece of information in a written material, without reading the whole text.

1. You must be focused. What you are looking for must be on your mind the whole time while scanning. Otherwise this will be a meaningless pursuit.
2. Before you start scanning trying to imagine in what form might the information appear. What are the words that it is most likely to be surrounded by?
3. Analyzing the content before you begin to scan is extremely important. For instance if you are about to scan material that you are familiar with, you would have no problem. However, if the material is pretty lengthy or hard for you to comprehend, then you might want to skim through it first, and then scan it.
4. Start scanning. Move your eyes from left to right very rapidly, quickly stopping when you bump into words that you think might appear in relation to the information you are looking for. It is recommended to scan a page for no longer than 15 seconds. As you become more experienced in this method you can reduce the time to 12, and then even 10 seconds.
5. When you find your information, read it.

Scanning is usually done at 1500 or more WPM.

Reading in Groups

We all learn to read word-by-word. There isn't really another way to do it. We learn to connect the syllables the right way so we can pronounce a real word. And while that may calls for a 'hooray' when you are 6 years old, reading word by word as an adult is definitely a disadvantage that may slow things down for you.

Instead of reading every word at a time, we must focus on learning how to read word groups. And though the previously mentioned techniques will improve your speed reading process a lot, I honestly don't think that anyone can learn to speed read if they don't know how to read a cluster of words at a single glance.

It is true that every word has a meaning. But when we are reading a sentence we have more than one word standing next to each other. Each of those words finds some 'partners' in the sentence with whom it forms a strong alliance – a word group. When you read every word separately you lose a lot of time. But being able to recognize the meaning of a word group in a split of a second will make you reach the end of a document lickety split.

Once you learn this method and combine it with some of the pacing techniques you can easily reach not only 700 WPM, but 900 as well.

But to do so, you must first be able to recognize word groups. Word groups are not just any group of word standing together. Word groups are the building blocks of a sentence. For instance, let's look at this example:

Your vacation home in Italy has the most amazing porch I have ever laid eyes on.

When you divide the sentence into meaningless clusters it may look something like this:

Your vacation home in

Italy has the most

Amazing porch

I have ever

Laid eyes on

As you can see, standing this way, none of these words have the meaning that the sentence carries. However, when you divide it into meaningful word groups, you will see how every group makes perfect sense:

Your vacation home

In Italy

has the most amazing porch

I have ever laid eyes on

To better understand the word groups, think of idioms for a second. Idioms are groups of words that has a single meaning. They are figure of speech that you immediately recognize, without even interpreting it. For instance, *a piece of cake* means *easy*. Try to see the word groups as idioms that carry a single meaning.

Learning to read groups of word at a single glance may increase your reading speed by incredible 300%. By doing so you:

- Extend your eye vision and decrease your eye fixation stops
- Improve your focus
- Ignore the filler words
- Focus on important nouns and verbs

Here is how you do it:

1. Start small. When learning how to read groups it is recommended to start reading shorter sentences at first.
2. Use your pacer. I recommend starting with your index finger.
3. Try to increase the reading speed and slow down where necessary to make sure that you comprehend the material.
4. Start with 15-minute exercises. You don't want to burden your eye muscles.
5. Do not judge yourself if you hear yourself whisper some words from time to time. It is normal. Just remember to use the counting exercise.

6. Once you can easily recognize groups, increase the timing.

7. Practice, practice and practice.

In-Depth Speed Reading

Another great strategy that will hasten your reading speed is in-depth reading. However, it is also the most complicated, and not to mention, the slowest one. But it is thorough. When you try to study a new piece of text, this is the best technique to try.

Why go through the trouble if it is the slowest technique, you must wonder. Well, let me ask you something. When you start reading a text you are unfamiliar with, can you possibly know at that moment that it will be absolutely relevant to your study? Or that it will not be a total waste of your time? Who says that the information isn't so dull that you will probably give up half way through? That is the linear approach to studying something, and it is by far the most inefficient way to use your time.

The in-depth reading is just the opposite of the linear approach. There are four main steps to in-depth reading:

1. Gathering the facts
2. Sorting the facts looking for importance and the correlation between them.
3. Measuring the facts against your previous knowledge
4. Selecting and separating the facts that you wish to remember from those you want to reject

Here is what happens when you want to use the in-depth speed reading:

Establishing the Purpose. Before reading you need to know your purpose. Why do I want to read this? How can I benefit from this material?

Survey. Before you decide to read a book (or other written material) you must first determine whether you want to use that material or not. The best way to do so is by skimming through the content. That will give you a clear picture of the main idea, which will tell you whether you can benefit from it or not.

In-Depth Studying. Keep in mind your main objective the whole time. Try reading as fast as you can, using the technique you find most suitable. The best reading guide is your main purpose why you chose to read that material, so do not forget that. Make notes all the time while you read. Use colored pencils that will help you underline keywords and important phrases. Do not be afraid to skip unimportant things or repetitive content. Keep in mind important questions like When What, Who, Why, Where and How, that will help you form a 'dialogue' between you and the material you are studying.

Evaluation. After speed reading the document, your thoughts must be organized. Remember the main part of the speed reading process is comprehension, so make sure that you have fully understood the written material.

Painting the Words

If you are like many people, then chances are you struggle to get enough interest for the topic you read about. That mainly happens because people fail to paint the words they read in their mind. If you choose to visually see the words you read, everything will be much different. You will have more interest, more understanding, and you will be more motivated to continue reading. When you have all of these, you can then master speed reading.

Pictures are much more powerful than words; just think about how easier it is to remember someone's face than it is to know his name. Same goes with reading. It is easier to concentrate if you can visually grasp the meaning of the context.

1. First, let's see if you have the ability to picture things in your mind. Imagine that you are laying down on the beach. Imagine you touching the sand, watching the waves crush. Now, imagine you standing up and taking a walk bare feet. Imagine your toes digging into the sand.

2. Now, take a book or any other reading material and read a single phrase or a sentence out loud. As soon as you read it, close your eyes and try to picture what you have just read. Be aware of the color, shape, as well as the distance of the picture.

3. Once you determine that you are perfectly able to paint the words in your mind, the next challenge is to see how capable of storing

multiple pictures you are. Read at least three and no more than 9 sentences that you can easily visualize. If you exceed your mental capacity of making pictures, you will most likely lose the first and last picture. When that happens you will know your number.

Although it may sound silly to you at this point, this exercise is actually the most effective way to improve your visualization ability. Make sure to practice the skill of picturing the words as often as you can. This will not only help you recognize the meaning of the text better, but it will also help you improve the focus and make you a better speed reader.

However, know that not any content is easy to visualize. For instance, it is not the same to picture a description of a house and some abstract material.

Advancing Your Speed-Reading Skills

Congratulations! You have learned what it takes to become a speed reader. However, unless you reinforce those abilities you may easily get disappointed. But don't worry. This chapter will tell you exactly what to do after you officially go beyond 700 WPM and how to remain on the speed reading track.

Expand Your Vocabulary. You cannot possibly understand what the author is trying to say if you don't know what the written words mean. That is why having a large vocabulary plays a major part in how fast of a reader you will be. The more words you know, the better you will understand the context, which means that, the faster you will read. Don't worry, I am not saying that you have to lock yourself in your room until you learn 500.000 words. However, if you want to advance your speed reading skills, then there are a couple of options you can try:

- Study a dictionary. When I say study, I don't mean memorizing verbs and nouns completely out of context. That will not expand your knowledge. To study a dictionary means to always check unknown words. For instance, if you read a book today and you come across a word that you don't know the meaning of, you take your dictionary and you look that word up. And since you will probably have to do this more than once in order to really memorize the word, it is highly recommended not to skip this step. That is studying a dictionary that can build your vocabulary.

- <u>Sound it out.</u> Sometimes you can understand the meaning of an unfamiliar word by simply sounding it out. Does it look like something that you know?
- <u>Determine the context.</u> The dictionary is not always a must. Sometimes you can determine the meaning of the word by simply considering the context of the sentence. The rest of the text can often help you figure out what a certain word means.

Try Speed Reading Software. We live in a digital world. So why not take advantage of all the technology that is around us? There are many great speed reading apps that will help you master the skill. The upside of the software learning is that everything is digital so you don't have to track your progress manually. The software will do all the work for you. And in case you don't know where to start, here are some ideas:

- <u>Spreeder</u> is a tool that gives you the opportunity of copying and pasting anything in a word processor. This tool then takes the text and turns it into an exercise. This app is amazing because it lets you choose what to read.
- <u>Accelerator</u> is an app that runs on iOS 8 that makes it possible for you to collect text and articles from different sources and import them into your speed reading tool. With this app you won't even feel like

practicing your speed reading, but simply reading an article of your choice.

- ReadMe! is an amazing app with great functionality that is especially appreciated by those speed readers who enjoy reading eBooks.

Practice Push-Up and Push-Down Exercises. The best way to enhance your ability to read with speed is actually quite simple:

- Push-Down Exercises are when you read the same material over and over again, but each time you try to read it in less time. For instance, let's imagine that you are about to read a 500-word text. The first time you read it in 75 seconds. The second time, you try to read it faster and you do it in 69. The third time you want to do it in 65. Then in 60 and so on. However, when doing this exercise you must remember that after each reading you have to answer the Who, What, When, How, Why, Where question. This will be an indicator of your progress. Your focus and comprehension must improve with each go-around.
- Push-Up Exercises are when you read the same material over and over again for the same amount of time, but each time trying to read more words. This exercise is done as a demonstrator of how faster it is to read something when you are already familiar with it.

Minimize the Eye Movement. Yes, it is possible to train that. For most people, the eyes cannot move in a single almost-fluid motion. They backtrack. If you spend some time observing your eye movements, you will notice how they move back and forth almost all the time. And while reading a single article that way may not make that much of a difference to you, in the long run, reading this way can waste hours and hours of your time. Fortunately, this can be trained. Here is an example that can help you do that:

- Try to keep your eyes as still as possible. When you move, keep your eyes looking forward. Even when your head moves, keep the eyes still. This will help you focus on a single phrase that you want to read slowly.
- Start moving your head from left to right, but keep your eyes centered and looking forward. They should not move with your head. This will help you create the almost-fluid eye motion.
- Now, do the opposite. Keep your head straight while looking from left to right with your eyes only. This is the key to speed reading lines without making too many movements.

Our head and eyes are tightly connected, but there are motions that one part does that do not affect the other. Make sure to practice this exercise as much as possible so you can become able to read smoothly.

Conclusion

Now that you have learned everything there is to know to become a speed reader, the next step is to simply implement those new skills and boost your efficiency.

This book will definitely help you perform your tasks more productively. And while I cannot guarantee that you will be the one to break the world's speed reading record (which is 4700 WPM by the way), I can definitely say that the methods within this book have helped many people increase their reading rate by 300%.

Now grab a book and let's get started.